Scott Foresman

Ten Important Sentences

Editorial Offices: Glenview, Illinois • Parsippany, New Jersey • New York, New York
Sales Offices: Needham, Massachusetts • Duluth, Georgia • Glenview, Illinois
Coppell, Texas • Sacramento, California • Mesa, Arizona

ISBN: 0-328-16901-3

5 6 7 8 9 10 V034 11 10 09 08 07

Contents

Unit 1:   Animal Friends

Unit 2:   Communities

Why Are Sentences So Important?

The sentence is the basic means of written communication. In order to be literate and articulate, students need to master sentence power.

When students read, they get information from sentences. Sentences provide facts and details, opinions, clues about the sequence of events, and information to understand cause and effect relationships. Students cannot get such meaning from sounds or words alone. Readers use sentences to build meaning in context and to decide on a main idea. You can think of the steps to comprehension as an inverted triangle, illustrating that comprehension is built upon the understanding that sounds create words that are parts of sentences which make up a text.

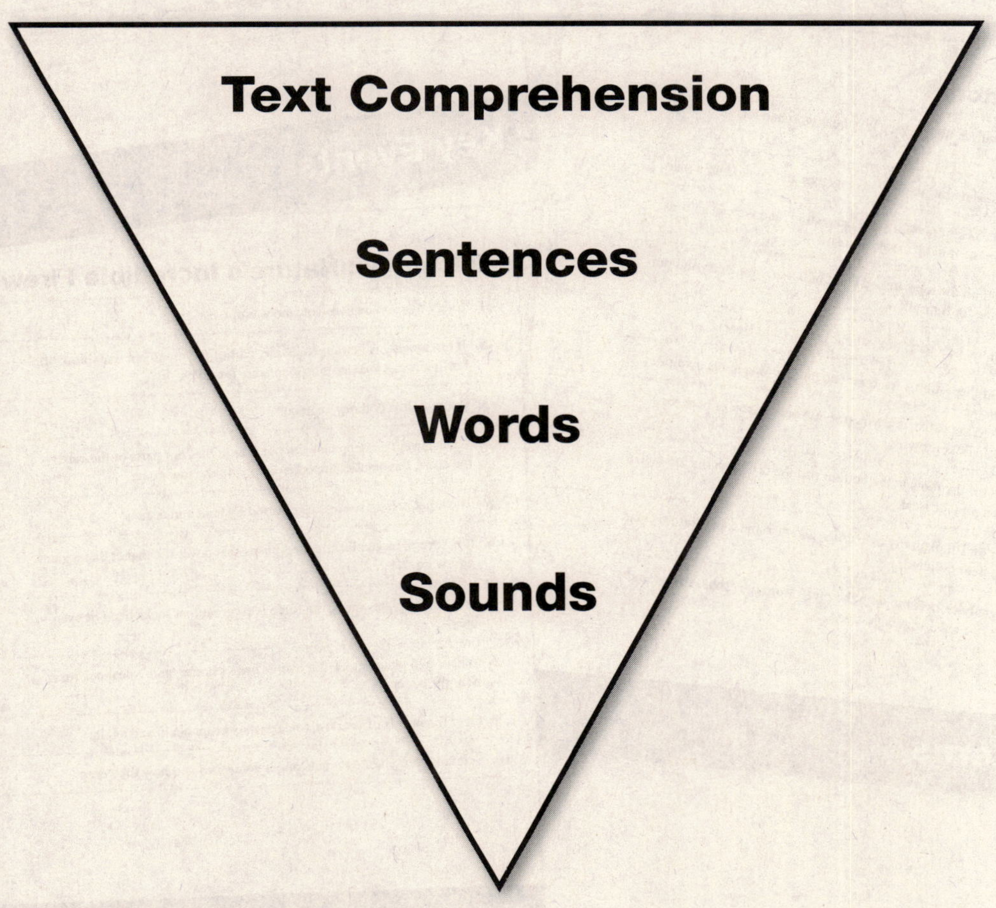

In this booklet, Ten Important Sentences are provided for every selection in the Student Edition. Each sentence is logical and cohesive; each sentence provides a key idea from the selection. Together, the Ten Important Sentences help students make meaning in several ways. Depending on the genre, Ten Important Sentences can do any of the following:

- Present **key events** in a story or narrative nonfiction selection such as a biography or autobiography

- Give the stated **main ideas and details** in an essay or informational selection, or

- Demonstrate a predictable **pattern** in a selection, for example in a song, poem, or nonsense story

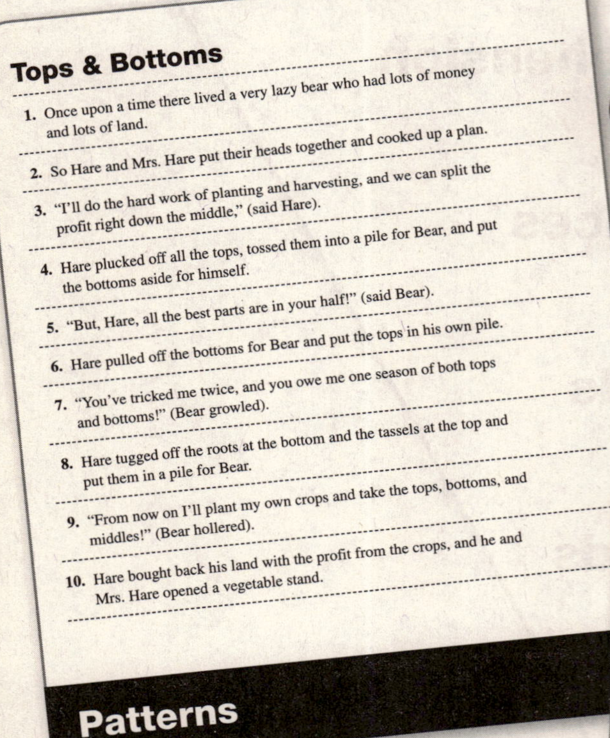

Gertrude Ederle

1. Gertrude Ederle was born on October 23, 1906.
2. She loved to swim.
3. By 1925 Trudy had set twenty-nine U.S. and world records.
4. She was determined to take on the ultimate challenge: the English Channel.
5. A newspaper editorial declared that Trudy wouldn't make it and that women must admit they would "remain forever the weaker sex."
6. She knew she would either swim the Channel or drown.
7. At about nine-forty at night, after more than fourteen hours in the water, Trudy's feet touched land.
8. She beat the men's record by almost two hours.
9. Reporters declared that the myth that women are the weaker sex was "shattered and shattered forever."
10. Gertrude Ederle had become a beacon of strength to girls and women everywhere.

Key Events

Tops & Bottoms

1. Once upon a time there lived a very lazy bear who had lots of money and lots of land.
2. So Hare and Mrs. Hare put their heads together and cooked up a plan.
3. "I'll do the hard work of planting and harvesting, and we can split the profit right down the middle," (said Hare).
4. Hare plucked off all the tops, tossed them into a pile for Bear, and put the bottoms aside for himself.
5. "But, Hare, all the best parts are in your half!" (said Bear).
6. Hare pulled off the bottoms for Bear and put the tops in his own pile.
7. "You've tricked me twice, and you owe me one season of both tops and bottoms!" (Bear growled).
8. Hare tugged off the roots at the bottom and the tassels at the top and put them in a pile for Bear.
9. "From now on I'll plant my own crops and take the tops, bottoms, and middles!" (Bear hollered).
10. Hare bought back his land with the profit from the crops, and he and Mrs. Hare opened a vegetable stand.

Patterns

Volcanoes: Nature's Incredible Fireworks

1. Every day somewhere volcanoes erupt.
2. If too much gas is trapped inside, part of the mountain may blow off, hurling rocks heavier than elephants for miles.
3. But not all volcanoes explode.
4. The answers lie deep beneath our feet in the four parts of the earth— the crust, the mantle, the outer core, and the inner core.
5. The crust, where we live, is covered by land and oceans.
6. It is several large pieces called plates that cover the planet like a giant jigsaw puzzle.
7. Where two plates meet, the force is so great that rocks bend or even break.
8. Where two plates meet, the mantle grows hotter, and volcanoes form near the edges.
9. Over thousands of years, a volcano may erupt again and again.
10. Scientists are learning what causes volcanoes and how they erupt.

Main Ideas and Details

How Ten Important Sentences Build Comprehension

Using and reusing *Ten Important Sentences* helps students build the skills they need for comprehension. *Ten Important Sentences* provides practical, selection-based instruction in these important skills:

- Recalling facts and details

- Finding and distinguishing between facts and opinions

- Arranging events in sequence

- Recognizing cause and effect relationships

- Identifying main idea and supporting details

You can help your students build their sentence power. Try these activities for building sentence power using *Ten Important Sentences*. The examples shown are from Grade 3. Match activities with other selections as you see fit.

Activity 1: Locate Sentences

1. Read the selection aloud to students or have students read all or parts of the selection silently.

2. Have students locate each of the Ten Important Sentences. (These will be those that tell the story or present the important ideas and details of the selection. The sentences on each master are in the correct order.) Discuss whether students agree with the choice of sentences. Which could they add or delete?

Activity 2: Distinguish Facts and Opinions

1. Read the selection aloud to students or have the students read all or parts of the selection silently. Discuss the selection, emphasizing sentences that are facts and sentences that are opinions.

2. Have students mark each of the Ten Important Sentences "F" for fact (something that can be proven) or "O" for opinion (something that a person believes or feels).

Me and Uncle Romie

1. Daddy thought it was a good time for me (James) to visit Uncle Romie and his wife, Aunt Nanette, up north in New York City. **F**

2. No, I wasn't sure about this visit at all. **O**

3. Home was like nothing I'd ever seen before. **O**

4. "Your uncle's working very hard, so we won't see much of him for a while" (said Aunt Nanette). **F**

5. My birthday was ruined. **O**

6. Looking at Uncle Romie's paintings, I could feel Harlem—its beat and bounce. **O**

7. "But the things we care about are pretty much the same" (said Uncle Romie). **O**

8. Uncle Romie held up two tickets to a baseball game! **F**

9. All these strangers talking to each other about their families and friends and special times, and all because of how my Uncle Romie's painting reminded them of things. **F**

10. And then I was off on a treasure hunt, collecting things that reminded me of Uncle Romie. **F**

Activity 3: Sequence Events

1. Read the selection aloud to students or have students read all or parts of the selection silently. Discuss the sequence of events, thoughts, or ideas in the selection.

2. Have students cut apart the Ten Important Sentences and mix the sentences in random order. Then have students order them correctly. (Note: Students can work with the sentences numbered or not, as you wish.)

Sequence

We all got together to build a church and a school.

Now this was a real boom town!

Activity 4: Link Cause and Effect

1. Read the selection aloud to students or have students read all or parts of the selection silently. Talk about events in the story and what causes them to happen.

2. Have students look at the Ten Important Sentences and find one or more pairs of sentences in which one sentence tells what happens and the other tells why it happens.

Cause

"There is more snow here than at home in England," said William.

Effect

He built a new roof with a very steep pitch and replaced the shingles.

Activity 5: Determine Main Idea

1. After reading, focus on the selection and talk with students about the big ideas.

2. Have students locate the sentences that provide the five elements of the main idea: who? did what? where? when? and why? Help students as they write the answers to these important questions in one sentence of their own.

Every day somewhere volcanoes erupt.

Notice that over time, students listen, manipulate sentences, and draw conclusions as they work toward comprehending what they have read. Using the Ten Important Sentences frees you from creating worksheets and lets you concentrate on helping students read and write with confidence.

x

The Main Idea Glove

Use the main idea glove to talk about the five elements of main idea. Duplicate this outline for each child or post it in your classroom. Your student will have the main idea right at hand!

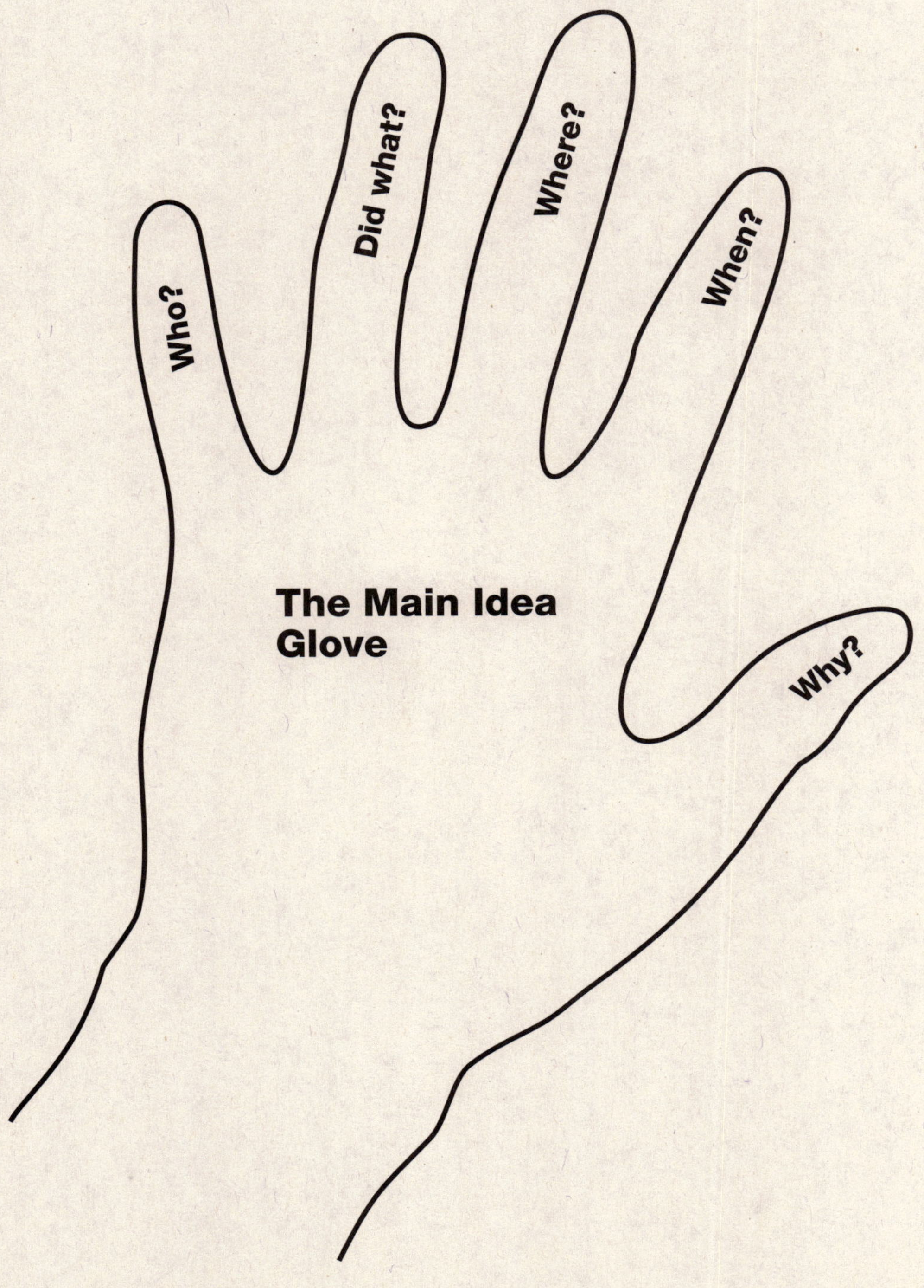

Sam, Come Back!

1. Sam the cat is on my lap.

2. Sam ran.

3. Sam, come back!

4. Sam ran that way.

5. See Sam in the sack.

6. Sam ran that way.

7. See Sam in the pack.

8. Sam, come back!

9. Sam is back.

10. Pat Sam on my lap.

Pig in a Wig

----

1. Pig in a wig is big, you see.

----

2. It is three.

----

3. Pig can mix.

----

4. Pig can lick.

----

5. It is six.

----

6. She is sick.

----

7. Fix that pig.

----

8. Take the sax!

----

9. Play it, Max, and play it, Pam!

----

10. Pig in a wig did a jig.

Ten Important Sentences • _Unit 1, Week 2_

The Big Blue Ox

1. Mom and Pop have a big blue ox.

2. Ox can help.

3. He can pick, and he can dig.

4. Pigs in wigs sit in mud.

5. Mop the pigs.

6. Off to town go Mom and Pop.

7. Hop on top.

8. Pack the sack.

9. Use big pans.

10. Mom and Pop nap on Ox.

A Fox and a Kit

1. This fox naps on the rocks.

2. Her kit naps on the rocks too.

3. The kit sits up.

4. The kit will eat.

5. The kit is licking his lips.

6. The kit nips and tags his mom.

7. The kit plays on the rocks.

8. His mom will get him.

9. The fox will watch her kit.

10. We like watching this kit and his mom too!

Get the Egg!

1. Kim saw Brad at the tree.

2. A big red bird is in the nest, Kim.

3. Six small eggs are in the nest too.

4. A big twig hit the nest!

5. Stop the egg, Brad.

6. You can help.

7. Get the egg in your net.

8. Set the egg back in the nest.

9. The big red bird is back, Kim.

10. Six small birds are in the nest too!

Animal Park

1. Camp is in a big, big park.

2. It is home to many animals.

3. We go bump, bump, bump in the truck.

4. A band of zebras runs past.

5. Big cats rest from a hunt.

6. Big birds stand in the grass.

7. Big hippos sit in mud.

8. Big elephants stand and sip in the pond.

9. We are back at camp.

10. We are glad we saw them!

© Pearson Education 1

A Big Fish for Max

1. "I wish I had a fish to eat," said Max.

2. "Then we will catch a big fish," said Grandma.

3. The path in the park led to the pond.

4. "Max can fish in this pond," said Ruby.

5. Max sat.

6. But no fish bit.

7. "Well, we can all walk to the fish shop," said Grandma.

8. The fish man had lots of fish in a box.

9. At home, Grandma put the fish in a hot pan.

10. "Yum, yum, yum!" said Max.

The Farmer in the Hat

1. "I could be the farmer, Old MacDonald, in this play," said Beth.

2. "No, I will be the farmer," said Dave.

3. "I have the hat!" said Max.

4. "Stop!" said Grace.

5. "We must make masks," (said Grace).

6. Max made a duck on his page.

7. Beth made hens.

8. Dave made a pig mask on his page.

9. "Take your places up on the stage," said Grace.

10. "Look at that cat!" said Grace.

Who Works Here?

1. People live and work in this neighborhood.

2. Who works in this place?

3. They all like to help us.

4. I make the neighborhood safe.

5. I help put out fires.

6. I put mail in your box.

7. I drive a big bus.

8. I pick up trash.

9. Who works where you live?

10. Smile at them.

The Big Circle

1. Big T. Rex wants meat to eat.

2. Here is a herd of triceratops.

3. "I'll get that baby," (said T. Rex).

4. The herd saw T. Rex run up and down.

5. They had time to make a big circle.

6. The small animals went inside the circle.

7. But T. Rex didn't quit.

8. They kept still in the big circle.

9. Together they drove him back.

10. Now they are safe.

Life in the Forest

1. We can find life all around the forest.

2. Sun shines on the leaves and helps them grow.

3. Many bugs like eating leaves.

4. The woodpecker pecks for bugs.

5. Small bugs made a home in the log.

6. The bird hops on the log and pecks at it.

7. Squirrels find the nuts and eat them.

8. The black bear eats leaves, grass, and nuts.

9. Hummingbirds can catch bugs for food too.

10. Many animals and plants call it home.

Honey Bees

1. In the family, there is a queen bee, many worker bees, and some drones.

2. She rules the hive.

3. Worker bees keep this hive safe.

4. Worker bees make wax cells in the hive.

5. Honey is food for bees.

6. Bees make honey from nectar.

7. Worker bees feed pollen to the queen bee and the little bees.

8. When those little bees get big, it is time for a new hive.

9. Worker bees make the new hive.

10. When it gets cold, the bees will go inside their hive to sleep and rest.

An Egg Is an Egg

1. A branch is a branch until it breaks.

2. And then it is a stick.

3. Nothing stays the same.

4. Everything can change.

5. This baby was a baby until he grew.

6. And now he is a boy.

7. But you can always be a baby.

8. You will always be my baby....

9. Some things stay the same.

10. Some things never change.

Ruby in Her Own Time

---

1. Once upon a time upon a nest beside a lake, there lived two ducks—a mother duck and a father duck.

---

2. Rufus, Rory, Rosie, and Rebecca swam off whenever they were able.

---

3. But Ruby swam nowhere.

---

4. "Will she ever swim?" said Father Duck.

---

5. "She will," said Mother Duck, "in her own time."

---

6. And—sure enough—she did.

---

7. And when Rufus, Rory, Rosie, and Rebecca began to fly... Ruby flew too!

---

8. She flew anywhere and everywhere.

---

9. "Will she ever come back?" said Mother Duck.

---

10. "She will," said Father Duck, "in her own time."

Ten Important Sentences • *Unit 3, Week 2*

Jan's New Home

1. Jan and her family must move away.

2. Jan is sad.

3. Our house, our school, our friends will change.

4. Jan packs her things, big and small, and takes her stuff down from the wall.

5. It is time to go.

6. This trip is fun!

7. Cars and buses are everywhere.

8. No more horses or tall yellow flowers.

9. This is our new home.

10. But the very best things are still the same.

Frog and Toad Together

1. "I wish I had a garden," said Toad.

2. He (Toad) planted the flower seeds.

3. The seeds did not start to grow.

4. "You are shouting too much," said Frog.

5. "Leave them alone for a few days," (said Frog).

6. Toad read a long story to his seeds.

7. And all the next day Toad played music for his seeds.

8. Then Toad felt very tired, and he fell asleep.

9. "Toad, Toad, wake up," said Frog.

10. Little green plants were coming up out of the ground.

I'm a Caterpillar

1. I'm a caterpillar.

2. I'm getting bigger!

3. I am a pupa.

4. I grow a shell to protect the pupa.

5. I am now a chrysalis.

6. I'm free!

7. I can fly!

8. I visit flowers.

9. Soon I will lay my eggs.

10. Baby caterpillars crawl out.

Where Are My Animal Friends?

1. Where is Caterpillar?

2. He became a chrysalis.

3. Then we won't see Caterpillar until spring when he'll be a butterfly.

4. I must fly away to where it is warm.

5. Yes, we'll be back in the spring.

6. I will see if Bear is at home.

7. I will sleep a long time.

8. All my friends are going away!

9. I will stay here all winter.

10. I have a warm nest and lots of food.

Mama's Birthday Present

1. "Next Sunday is Mama's birthday!" (said Francisco).

2. "If we begin today, we will have seven days to plan a party," (said Grandma).

3. "What present can I give Mama?" (asked Francisco).

4. "We can make a piñata to break," (said Grandma).

5. "I can play my guitar," (said Papa).

6. "I can bring some hot tortillas, fresh off the stove," (said Señora Molina).

7. "We can make confetti eggs to crack on people's heads," (said Gina).

8. "We can make some sweet buñuelos," (said Grandpa Pérez)

9. "I did not know what to give you for your birthday, Mama," (said Francisco).

10. "The best present of all is having my family and friends here with me," (said Mama).

The Dot

1. "I just CAN'T draw!" (said Vashti).

2. "Just make a mark and see where it takes you," (said the teacher).

3. She (the teacher) pushed the paper toward Vashti and quietly said, "Now sign it."

4. The next week, when Vashti walked into art class, she was surprised to see what was hanging above her teacher's desk.

5. Vashti painted and painted.

6. At the school art show a few weeks later, Vashti's many dots made quite a splash.

7. Vashti noticed a little boy gazing up at her.

8. "I wish I could draw," he (the boy) said.

9. She (Vashti) handed the boy a blank sheet of paper.

10. And then she (Vashti) said…"Sign it."

Mister Bones

---

1. Smooth Barnum Brown was a charming, dapper guy.

---

2. Mister Brown came to Montana in a fancy coat and hat.

---

3. He poked and he sifted and he picked in the dirt.

---

4. But what he hunted, people wanted just about as much as gold.

---

5. People said, "Barnum Brown can somehow smell bones."

---

6. His nickname became Mister Bones.

---

7. Mister Bones found bones in the middle of Montana—a backbone and a hip bone and other bones and chips.

---

8. Bones were packed in boxes, shipped off to New York.

---

9. Putting them together took lots and lots of work.

---

10. Mister Bones had found the tyrant lizard king.

The Lady in the Moon

1. It is Moon Festival, a night for children everywhere.

2. Night is falling, and children call, "Come out, Lady Moon."

3. High above the city, high above the hills, the moon shows her golden face.

4. Children sing and laugh.

5. She glows, she glides, she grows.

6. Lady Moon fills the sky with light.

7. The moon is so near, you can touch it if you try.

8. We light our lanterns.

9. We raise them high.

10. Let's laugh and sing a song to Lady Moon.

Peter's Chair

1. "Remember, we have a new baby in the house," (said mother).

2. "That's my cradle," he (Peter) thought, "and they painted it pink!"

3. "Let's run away, Willie," he (Peter) said.

4. They went outside and stood in front of his house.

5. He arranged his things very nicely and decided to sit in his chair for a while.

6. But he couldn't fit in the chair.

7. But Peter got an idea.

8. Soon his mother saw signs that Peter was home.

9. Peter sat in a grown-up chair.

10. "Daddy," said Peter, "let's paint the little chair pink for Susie."

Henry and Mudge

1. On this Valentine's Day, Henry's father and Henry's mother were going to a Sweetheart Dance.

2. Henry and Mudge would be staying with Mrs. Hopper.

3. Mrs. Hopper lived across the street in a big stone house with droopy trees and dark windows and a gargoyle on the door.

4. Mrs. Hopper wasn't like anyone Henry had ever met.

5. She played the violin for him.

6. She told him about her father, who had been a famous actor.

7. She was very kind to Mudge.

8. After the tea and music and oatmeal, Mrs. Hopper took them upstairs.

9. Henry and Mudge and Mrs. Hopper spent most of the evening in the costume room.

10. They had a wonderful time.

Tippy-Toe Chick, Go!

----

1. Every morning when the dew had dried, Hen took her chicks to the garden for their favorite treat—sweet itty-bitty beans and potato bugs.

----

2. A big, grumpy dog came running their way, barking and growling at the end of a rope.

----

3. Big Chick ran to hide under Hen's safe wing.

----

4. Little Chick peeped, "*I* want to try."

----

5. "You're much too small," (said Hen).

----

6. And off she went, tippy-toe, tippy-toe, as fast as she could.

----

7. Hen screamed and grabbed her heart.

----

8. Dog's rope was wrapped all around the tree.

----

9. Big Chick and Middle Chick just stood and stared.

----

10. Little Chick called, "It's time to eat!"

Mole and the Baby Bird

1. Mole found a baby bird.

2. Mole waited and waited: but no big bird came to help it—so Mole took the baby bird home.

3. "It mustn't fly!" (cried Mole).

4. "I'm making a cage for my pet bird!" said Mole.

5. The bird was sad.

6. Grandad took Mole to the top of a high hill.

7. "I'm flying!" cried Mole.

8. He opened the cage door, and he let his bird fly away because he loved it.

9. Then he cried.

10. He saw his bird flying, soaring, free.

Dot & Jabber

1. "We need a mystery to solve," said Jabber.

2. "What is this little oak tree doing here?" (asked Dot).

3. "Acorns are oak tree seeds," (said Jabber).

4. "Let's look for clues," (said Dot).

5. "How did our acorn get from there to here?" (asked Jabber).

6. The detectives set off across the meadow.

7. A squirrel came and sat down among the acorns.

8. When the squirrel stopped, they stopped and watched to see what would happen next.

9. "Our acorn crossed the meadow on squirrel feet," (said Dot).

10. "We are two clever mouse detectives!" (said Dot).

Simple Machines

1. Machines help make our lives easier.

2. Some levers can help you move a heavy object, such as a rock.

3. One side goes up, while the other side goes down.

4. An inclined plane is a flat surface that is slanted.

5. It is easier to push a big load up a ramp than to lift it.

6. Wheels help things go.

7. An axle, or rod, connects a pair of wheels.

8. It would be very hard work to move a bike or car without wheels.

9. A pulley helps you lift heavy objects.

10. A pulley's rope passes over a small wheel.

Alexander Graham Bell

----

1. Alexander Graham Bell was born in Scotland in 1847.

----

2. Alexander was good at music and science.

----

3. In 1871, Alexander moved to Boston.

----

4. During the day, he taught deaf students how to speak.

----

5. In 1874, he met Tom Watson.

----

6. He and Tom wanted to invent a machine that could send voices from one place to another.

----

7. Alexander spoke to Tom through the first telephone.

----

8. In 1915, they made the first telephone call across the United States.

----

9. He died in 1922.

----

10. Alexander Graham Bell changed the way people communicate with one another.

Ben Franklin and His First Kite

1. It was a rare day indeed when Ben did not have a plan in mind.

2. "I want to try an experiment at the millpond," (said Ben).

3. He ran to get the kite he had made the week before.

4. "But that kite is nothing special," (said one boy).

5. "The invention is what I'm going to do with it," (said Ben).

6. "I'm going to cross this pond without swimming a stroke," (said Ben).

7. The wind tugged on the kite.

8. The boys whooped and hollered as Ben glided across the pond.

9. "What will you do next?" they (the boys) asked.

10. But he was sure he would think of something.